I Will See You in Heaven, My Friend

The Bible Tells Me So!

DANNA HOMAN

WestBow Press books may be ordered through booksellers or by contacting:

WestBow Press
A Division of Thomas Nelson & Zondervan
1663 Liberty Drive
Bloomington, IN 47403
www.westbowpress.com
1 (866) 928-1240

ISBN: 978-1-9736-5645-6 (sc)
ISBN: 978-1-9736-5646-3 (e)

Library of Congress Control Number: 2019902805

Print information available on the last page.

WestBow Press rev. date: 04/03/2019

WESTBOW
PRESS®
A DIVISION OF THOMAS NELSON
& ZONDERVAN

INTRODUCTION

"ARE ANIMALS IN HEAVEN?"

Losing a precious pet is an experience that leaves us in total grief and searching for consolation and peace.

I love the saying *"Until one has loved an animal, a part of one's soul remains unawakened"* by Anatole France.

It's so true! But when we lose them, a part of our soul is just gone. Their absence leaves a gaping hole that seems impossible to fill.

When I lost my own precious Sadie in 2014, way too early at just eight years old, I was completely unable to get my arms around it. She had been my little sidekick for eight years and losing her too soon was something for which I wasn't prepared.

I needed peace.

I needed to believe that she was in Heaven and that we would see each other again. Everyone talked of the "Rainbow Bridge," which is such a beautiful thought, but I am a Bible believing Christian and the only thing that brings me total peace is the Word of my Father. That led me to look up all references to 'rainbow' in the Bible.

Although there was no mention of a "Rainbow Bridge," what I DID find which I wasn't aware of before, is that the rainbow covenant that God made with Noah WASN'T just to mankind, but to 'every living creature' that was with him! It was a covenant between God and ALL of His creation!

So what exactly is a 'covenant?'

Bible-Researcher.Com defines covenant this way:

"The Greek word διαθηκη (diatheke), usually translated "covenant" in English versions of the Bible, is a legal term denoting a formal and legally binding declaration of benefits to be given by one party to another, with or without conditions attached." [1]

God made a promise to animals!

Not a passing, changeable, fickle promise. But an ETERNAL, binding promise!

If they are temporary, why would He make a promise to them?

If He didn't love them, why would He make this everlasting covenant with them? Not a temporary promise, but an ETERNAL one.

That got me so excited that it inspired my journey to start at Genesis
and walk through the entire Bible to see what God says.

There's man's 'opinion' which is usually based on emotion, and then there's
the truth of the Word of God. I prayed that He would open my eyes to the
truth, and it was in this journey that God revealed His faithfulness and
love, not just to me and all of mankind, but to the animals that clearly bring
Him much joy. As we are created in His image, I now see that He gets as
much joy from this aspect of His creation as we do! What a happy thought!

I get asked this question so often that I decided to share the
answer, and I hope that it blesses all who read it.

I wrote this in a way you can follow along in the Scriptures for yourself
and come to your own conclusion. But in reading this, I hope you find
peace and the ability to draw upon the Scriptures when God puts
you in a position to provide love and compassion to someone else.

Now the fun part begins.

Let's walk through God's word together and witness how much
He loves ALL of His Creation! Let us observe the eternal
plan He has for every single aspect of that Creation.

I'm going to ask you some questions, and I would challenge you to
follow along with me in your Bible to come to your own conclusions.

Remember, God is the same yesterday, today and
tomorrow. He is eternal...not temporary.

May your eyes be opened now and forever as you see Him in EVERYTHING!!

Proverbs 12:10, NIV

"The righteous care for the needs of the animals, but
the kindest acts of the wicked are cruel."

Why would our Father call it 'righteous' to care for
animals if He didn't care about them????

We are created in His image and were given an awesome
responsibility to care for all of which God entrusted to us. So I
am ever amazed when someone asks me how I can be "so sure"
that God loves animals and that they are in Heaven.

I understand the question from those who don't consider the Bible to be the
eternal, inerrant Word of God; however, for those who do call themselves
"believers," how can one "claim" to love the Lord and not love everything He
loves? How can one "claim" to know the Scriptures and ever doubt that God
has an eternal plan, not just for mankind, but for ALL of His Creation?

How can God speak life into something, bless it, and call it
"good," yet man has come to the conclusion that it isn't?

Or that it isn't valuable to the Creator?

Or that it's temporary?

God is a God of the eternal…not the temporary.

Author and Biblical scholar Gary Kurz says in his book, "Cold Noses
at the Pearly Gates," 'God is not a God of the temporary. He does
not make things on a temporary basis…' Yes, man is created in His

image and there's no disputing the incredible importance of that; however, God also loves every single aspect of His creation. [2]

God is very clear throughout Scripture how important animals are to Him.

In Genesis 1:31, "God saw everything that He had made, and indeed it was very good."

Not just good, but VERY good.

Gary Kurz states it this way and I believe it to be profound – "He was very happy with His work and with the relationship He had orchestrated between mankind and animals. Lest we forget who we are talking about here, it was GOD who did the work and GOD who made the assessment." [3]

2.

Did you know that in the beginning, when God created the earth and all that was in it, there was no bloodshed?

No predator.

No hunter and the hunted.

And it was as God intended.

It was perfect.

It was His will on earth, as it was in Heaven. The Garden was Heaven on earth. God walked with Adam and Eve. The animals co-existed with man. God provided for ALL of His creation.

Man and animal were only given permission to eat that which was provided by the earth.

Genesis 1:29-30 *CJB*, Then God said, "Here! Throughout the whole earth I am giving you as food every seed-bearing plant and every tree with seed-bearing fruit. And to every wild animal, bird in the air and creature crawling on the earth, in which there is a living soul, I am giving as food every kind of green plant. And that is how it was." [4]

Interesting, right?

Animals were not 'created' for us to eat as some have wrongly assumed. And the Bible makes it clear that every creature on earth has a soul.

3.

So, when did man start to eat flesh for food?

It wasn't until Genesis chapter 9, after the great flood, that
God gave Noah permission for men to eat flesh.

...AFTER THE FLOOD...

After man's sinful nature got so bad that all of creation was destroyed in
the flood, with the exception of the remnant that God preserved in the ark.

Again, don't take my word for it. Read for yourself in Genesis 9:3 NIV:

*"Everything that lives and moves about will be food for you. Just
as I gave you the green plants, now I give you everything."*

'NOW I give you everything...'

Until that point, both man and animal had been provided
for throughout the earth with every seed-bearing plant
and every tree with every seed-bearing fruit.

To this day, some of the strongest and most magnificent creatures on
earth are vegetarian. The Elephant, Gorilla, Giraffe, Deer, Rhino, Bison
and Hippo, only to name a few, still only eat what the earth provides.

We know that in the end, Eden will be restored, as God intended!

The way we were all created to live…
IN HARMONY!

Isaiah 11:6-9

"The wolf also shall dwell with the lamb, the leopard shall lie down with the young goat, the calf and the young lion and the fatling together; and a little child shall lead them.

The cow and the bear shall graze, their young ones shall lie down together, and the lion shall eat straw like the ox.

The nursing child shall play by the cobra's hole, and the weaned child shall put his hand in the viper's den.

They shall not hurt nor destroy in all My holy mountain, for the earth shall be full of the knowledge of the Lord as the waters cover the sea."

To quote Gary Kurz once again:

"…God never changes and what He planned in the beginning,
even though temporarily offset by mankind's disobedience
is not lost. He will bring His perfect will to pass." [5]

4.

Did you know that every animal that harms a man
will have to give 'an accounting' to God?

Yes…an accounting!

In Genesis 9:4-5 *NIV* God goes on to tell Noah that He
will demand an accounting 'from every animal.'

"But you must not eat meat that has its lifeblood still in it. And for
your lifeblood I will surely demand an accounting. I will demand
an accounting from every animal. And from each man, too, I
will demand an accounting for the life of one's fellow man."

How can an animal give an accounting to God if it is not WITH God?

5.

As I briefly mentioned in the Introduction, did you know that the rainbow covenant was not just between God and man, but between God and 'every living creature of every kind on the earth?'

Genesis 9:9-10
"And as for Me, behold, I establish My covenant with you and with your descendants after you, and with every living creature that is with you: the birds, the cattle, and every beast of the earth with you, of all that go out of the ark, every beast of the earth."

Genesis 9:12-15
And God said: "This is the sign of the covenant which I make between Me and you, and every living creature that is with you, for perpetual generations: I set My rainbow in the cloud, and it shall be for the sign of the covenant between Me and the earth. It shall be, when I bring a cloud over the earth, that the rainbow shall be seen in the cloud; and I will remember My covenant which is between Me and you and every living creature of all flesh; the waters shall never again become a flood to destroy all flesh."

God included animals in His everlasting promise!!!
If they are temporary, why would He have done that?

I think it is very interesting that God repeats the rainbow covenant TWICE!
Back to back.

He doesn't repeat things unless He really wants us to pay attention!
So the next time you see a rainbow, and every time thereafter, remember all to whom that promise was made!

6.

Did you know that the original Hebrew text for
'dominion' actually means *stewardship?*"

So just what is the definition of 'stewardship?"

Merriam-Webster Dictionary defines the word as this:
The conducting, supervising, or managing of something. [6]

Dictionary.Com defines it even better:
*The responsible overseeing and protection of something
considered worth caring for and preserving.* [7]

It is true that God gave man dominion over the animals, but
what an awesome responsibility that is! By this definition,
we are to manage and care for God's creation!
They are worth caring for and preserving!
God's animals. Not ours.

"For, the Earth is the Lord's and everything in it"
1 Corinthians 10:26 *NIV*

Where in Scripture does 'dominion' equal 'neglect' or 'cruelty?'

Or selfish gain?

Or to take advantage of?

Or to disrespect?

Is this thought process just because God gave man dominion over them?

I want to refer to an article by Kristen Swenson, Ph.D and author of
God and Earth: Discovering a Radically Ecological Christianity.

The article appeared in HUFFPOST on 8/14/2010 and is entitled,
"The Bible and Human 'Dominion' Over Animals:
Superiority or Responsibility?"

"… in this biblical story, human superiority brings not self-serving
privilege but grave responsibility…Human beings have the unique
responsibility, then, to work creatively at maintaining an order
that allows each thing to be and do all of what it is and does.
And that, this first chapter in Genesis declares, is good." [8]

And that, God declares…
"is good."

7.

Have you ever thought about why animals were the ONLY means of atonement and forgiveness in the Old Testament?

Because animals are perfect and sinless.

Adam and Eve ate of the fruit. And sin entered the world.
Man was separated from God.

Animals never veered from the state in which they were created.

Only mankind.

And only mankind needed to be reconciled to the Father.

Animals never lost their eternal innocence.

So before the one perfect and sinless Savior came to die for the sins of all mankind, the sacrificial system with animals was the only way.

Many wonder that if God loved animals so much, why
He would allow animals to be sacrificed.

Because He loves us too much NOT to allow it.

He makes that love clear in the New Testament.

John 3:16
"For God so loved the world, that He gave His only begotten Son, that whosoever believeth in Him should not perish but have everlasting life."

GOD LOVES THE WORLD! And before He gave His only Son to die for us, animals were the only way for reconciliation.

Before Jesus, the sacrificial Lamb of the New Testament, the animal sacrifices only "covered" the sins of man. The first time God introduces this is in Genesis 3:21:

"Unto Adam also and to his wife did the Lord God make coats of skins, and clothed them."

Adam and Eve sinned and Eden was lost. For the first time, they recognized their nakedness, so God had to clothe them from head to toe so they could stand in His presence.

Because of sin...
He covered them.

From that point on, the Hebrews had to sacrifice a perfectly clean animal in order to reconcile themselves to God.

And it had to be perfect.

An animal was the only thing that could be perfect and without blemish.

For the final reconciliation of mankind to our Father, His son was the only perfect sacrifice that could be made.

John the Baptist testified to this truth when he cried out, *"...Behold, the Lamb of God, which taketh away the sin of the world!"* John 1:29

Not only would Jesus "cover" our sin, as the animal sacrifices had done up until that time, but He would take sin away.

TAKE IT AWAY!!

Jesus, The Lamb of God.

The FINAL LAMB.

And it was finished.

1 Corinthians 5:7, *"...For Christ, our Passover lamb, has been sacrificed."* NIV

And did you know that the crucifixion took place in Jerusalem during Passover, the exact time that the Jewish people sacrificed their own Passover lambs? [9]

God's timing is never accidental.

And it's always perfect.

8.

Did you know that the Bible tells us about a
Donkey that God allowed to talk?!

In Numbers 22:21-23, we are told the story of Balaam's Donkey. To
paraphrase, God was angry with Balaam for disobeying Him, so He
put an angel in the road to oppose him on his journey. Now Balaam
was riding the donkey, who could see the angel standing in the road
with a drawn sword. The donkey could literally see the angel!!

However, Balaam and his two servants could not see the angel. The
donkey swerved off the road three times to avoid the angel. Each time
Balaam beat her. After the third beating, Numbers 22:28 NIV tells us,
"Then the Lord opened the donkey's mouth, and it said to Balaam,
"What have I done to make you beat me these three times?" Then the
Lord opened Balaam's eyes to see the angel. When this happened,
Balaam fell facedown. Then the angel said, "The donkey saw me and
turned away from me these three times. If she had not turned away, I
would certainly have killed you by now, but I would have spared her."

A talking donkey! Intriguing!

This donkey saw the angel and swerved out of the way, not once, not twice,
but three times. Because she could see the angel, she saved Balaam's life.

9.

Did you know the Bible tells us that God
preserves BOTH people and animals?

Psalm 36:6 NIV
*"Your righteousness is like the highest mountains, your justice like
the great deep. You, Lord, preserve both people and animals."*

Why does the Bible tell us that God preserves
both if they're not both in Heaven?

10.

The book of Job is filled with lessons God teaches using animals.

Did you know that not only is mankind in His protective
hand, but also the life of every creature?

Job 12:10

"In whose hand is the soul of every living thing and the breath of all mankind."

So here we are again where the Word of God tells us that every living
thing DOES have a soul! How magnificent to understand! One only has
to look into the eyes of any animal to see how true this really is. Clearly
our Creator gets magnificent joy in their existence. As should we!!!

Job addressed the importance of paying attention to the animal saying,

"Ask the animals and they will teach you"
Job 12:7-12 NIV

God uses animals for SUCH amazing purposes in this world!!

They teach us so much about spirituality. All throughout the Bible, and still today, God uses the natural world to teach us spiritual truths.

Because it is the only way our minds can understand His greatness.

Animals are a huge part of this!

They are the epitome of unconditional love and devotion, forgiveness and complete joy...with nothing more than being in the presence of loved ones. They can warn us when danger is near. They can help us anticipate the weather. They can sense the presence of disease. They can thwart bombings. They can rescue people from places humans cannot or will not go.

I agree with Job. Just think about all the lessons animals teach us? If we would just pay attention.

"When loved ones come home, always run to greet them.
Never pass up the opportunity to go for a joyride.
Allow the experience of fresh air and the wind in your face to be pure ecstasy.
When you're happy, dance around and wag your entire body.
Delight in the simple joy of a long walk.
Be loyal.
Never pretend to be something you're not.
When someone is having a bad day, be silent, sit
close by, and nuzzle them gently." [10]

And an animal will most certainly die for its human. No doubt about it.

God will open the eyes of your heart to see Him in ALL of His Creation – if only you have the faith like a child to ask, and to observe, and to learn.

His Creation is the greatest love story ever written.

Paul says in Colossians 1:16-17

"For by Him all things were created that are in heaven and that are on earth, visible and invisible, whether thrones or dominions or principalities or powers. All things were created through Him and for Him. And He is before all things, and in Him all things consist."

Do you think repeating it four times is enough to make the point that "all things" are of God and are created for Him?

I certainly get the point, do you?

David states that
"The earth is the Lord's, and everything in it."
Psalm 24:1 NIV

Not 'some things,' but EVERYTHING in it.

11.

In the book of 2 Kings, we are told the story of Elisha, who was a prophet and protector of Israel, and his servant. The king of the Arameans sent an army to capture them. When Elisha and his servant were faced with what 'seemed' to be a hopeless defeat by this enemy's army, the servant was very afraid. Elisha prayed that God would open his servant's eyes so that he could see the power that was with them.

And what did God do?

When Elisha prayed, God revealed to the servant that they were surrounded by angel armies of horses and chariots of fire!!
2 Kings 6:17

Horses are in God's own army!! If animals are not in
Heaven, where do the horses come from?

12.

Did you know that ALL of Creation will sing His praises?!!

ALL CREATION will praise our Creator!
Not just mankind. ALL CREATION.

Psalm 96:11-13 NIV
"Let the heavens rejoice, let the earth be glad; let the sea resound, and all that is in it. Let the fields be jubilant, and everything in them; let all the trees of the forest sing for joy. Let all creation rejoice before the Lord, for he comes, He comes to judge the earth. He will judge the world in righteousness and the peoples in his faithfulness."

Think about that for a moment. Bunnies, squirrels, cows, elephants, zebras, horses, fish, birds and lions! ALL that is on the earth will rejoice when Jesus comes back at the appointed time! Even the trees!!! Just close your eyes for a moment and think about that. The WONDER of that.

13.

How does Jesus return in majesty and glory?

On a white horse!!!

In Revelation 19:11-16, when Jesus returns gloriously at the appointed time, Scripture tells us that He will be riding a white horse!

*Again, if animals are not part of the heavenly
realm, from where does the horse come?*

Animals were there in the beginning,
AND
they will be there in the end!!

According to God!!

Revelation 5:13
"And every creature which is in heaven and on the earth and under the earth and such as are in the sea, and all that are in them, I heard saying: "Blessing and honor and glory and power be to Him who sits on the throne, And to the Lamb, forever and ever!"

JUST IMAGINE THAT!!!

EVERY CREATURE praising Jesus TOGETHER!

So, I've posed and answered twelve questions about God's eternal plan for animals. If you still want more, let's see what else His Word says about this magnificent aspect of His Creation.

Matthew 10:29 and Luke 12:6 tell us that God knows EVERY single time a sparrow falls!

He has his eye on even the smallest of His creation! Not even a sparrow can fall to the ground without God knowing it.

God called forth fish in the sea, birds in the air and animals on the land...

and

He called it *GOOD*.

The most powerful proof to me of how much God loves His animal
kingdom is that He used them to describe His SON!

"The Lion of Judah"
And
"The Lamb of God."

He also used the Dove as an illustration of the
Holy Spirit when Jesus got baptized.

And other than Mary and Joseph, who else
surrounded Jesus when He was born?
God sent His precious son to us via a stable, surrounded by animals.

They were there in the beginning when God created
them, spoke life into them and called them good.

They were there throughout the Old Testament.

They were there throughout the New Testament.

And most importantly, they were there at the birth of the Savior.

They will be there when Jesus returns.

And they will be there in Heaven. When Eden is restored
and the wolf will lie down with the lamb.

God is the same yesterday, today and tomorrow.

He doesn't change.

My prayer is that people will be driven to the Scriptures for greater clarity and wisdom when forming any opinions on any subject. And in doing so, one will be amazed at how one's relationship with the Father will be refined.

Throughout the Bible, Jesus used parables of the natural so that people could understand the spiritual. I hope you too will start to see Him in ALL ASPECTS of His majestic Creation. For He is GOOD, and it is GOOD! He is The Maker of all and Lover of all.

May the Holy Creator of the universe, the Master Architect and Lover of all His creation bless and keep you. May He make His face to shine upon you and be gracious to you; may the Lord turn His face toward you and give you peace. Peace that when you have to say 'goodbye' to your furry family in this life, that it is only for a little while…goodbye 'for now,' until you see each other again. And peace that God now has them in HIS hands; for the Bible tells us so!

For He is GOOD.
And it is GOOD.

ARTWORK BY OLIVIA LOVE

EPILOGUE

My Sadie. She wasn't a rescue, so I can't attribute some remarkable survival story to her. But what I CAN attribute to her is teaching me all about the magnificent power of animals and those in need of our help.

Never forget that God can use ANYTHING to
help mankind understand His love.

All throughout Scripture, Jesus used parables, or stories about the natural world, to help His followers understand Biblical truths. And for many people in the world, the love of an animal may be the only example of true, unconditional love that they ever experience. Who are we to belittle that?

It was in having Sadie that I got involved in animal rescue. And it was my Sadie that taught all my other rescues how to adjust and become the dogs they were meant to be. She was a beacon of light and lessons in my life until we had to say goodbye when she was only eight years old.

In the journey with my Father after her loss, I realized that He loved her too! Sadie was on assignment. He gave her to me! My life was forever changed. God used her to refine my heart. He used her to teach me so much more about Him. And through Sadie, my journey with my Heavenly Father took a path much deeper than I could've ever imagined. And her job was done. I was ready to go at it alone, and Sadie was ready to go home. He loved her first and He loved her best. And He has her until we see each other again! As traumatic as losing her was, her love lives on in the lives of all the others that have been saved because she lived.

My Sadie...what a glorious dog she was! With such a special assignment in this world! Thank you for sharing in our journey and I hope your heart was blessed.

If you want to read about my own survival story with Sadie
and my little puppy mill rescue, Molly, you can go to

https://www.guideposts.org/friends-and-family/pets/
service-animals/a-courageous-heart-like-molly-s

"A Courageous Heart Like Molly's"
"She thought she had rescued the fearful little dog,
but it turned out to be the other way around"

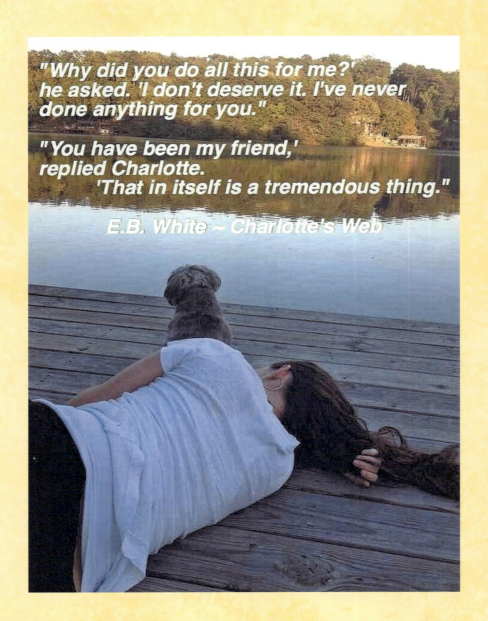

"Why did you do all this for me?' he asked. 'I don't deserve it. I've never done anything for you."

"You have been my friend,' replied Charlotte. 'That in itself is a tremendous thing."

E.B. White ~ Charlotte's Web

BIBLIOGRAPHY

1. https://www.bible-researcher.com/covenant.html
2. Kurz, Gary. *"Cold Noses at the Pearly Gates."* Citadel Press. Kensington Publishing Corp. 2008
3. Kurz, Gary. *"Cold Noses at the Pearly Gates."* Citadel Press. Kensington Publishing Corp. 2008
4. Complete Jewish Bible. Genesis 1:29-30
5. Kurz, Gary. *"Cold Noses at the Pearly Gates."* Citadel Press. Kensington Publishing Corp. 2008
6. Merriam-Webster Dictionary
7. https://www.dictionary.com/browse/stewardship
8. Swenson, Kristin. *"The Bible and Human 'Dominion' Over Animals: Superiority or Responsibility?"* HUFFPOST, 14 Aug, 2010. https://www.huffingtonpost.com/kristin-m-swenson-phd/the-bible-and-human-domin_b_681363.html
9. Luke 22:7 NIV (See Note: The Passover Lamb had to be sacrificed on the 14th of Nisan between 2:30 and 5:30 P.M. in the court of the priests – Thursday of Passion Week)
10. Author Unknown. Excerpt from *"A Dog's Purpose? Explained By a 6-Year-Old"*
11. Artwork by Olivia Love, Tupelo, MS. "Max The One-Eared Wonder Dog and His Human, Riley Mulrooney"

Printed in the United States
By Bookmasters